Laughter from the Hive

Voor Tonnie Bakkenist
met liefde

Laughter from the Hive

KATE FOLEY

Shoestring Press

Acknowledgements

Some of these poems have been published, sometimes in different versions, by The Interpreters House, Scintilla, Second Light, DVoice and Versal.

Typeset and printed by Q3 Print Project Management Ltd, Loughborough, Leics
(01509 213456)

Published by Shoestring Press
19 Devonshire Avenue, Beeston, Nottingham, NG9 1BS
(0115) 925 1827
www.shoestringpress.co.uk

First published 2004
© Copyright: Kate Foley
The moral right of the author has been asserted.
ISBN: 1 904886 01 9

Shoestring Press gratefully acknowledges financial assistance from Arts Council England

Contents

ZIN

If you find yourself devouring poetry
like a box of chocolates

endorphins kicking in, a cocaine rush,
more a bubble of spit

forming at the corner of your mouth
preceding thought, memory, digestion,

if love is met by a lover, whose need
is so equal and opposite

that you both stand up in your post-piranha
bones and if you swallow god,

not in Its little, light, algebraic bread
jacket but as if It were food

for hollow mountains, then you need
the trenchant lexicography

of another language. The Dutch
say 'zin' for more than appetite,

a word so herring-salty it can be used for love
but not bulimia.

I should not dare to find an African word
for hunger, food

or love but if I could pray, I would
before I die: let me learn,

let me learn to eat slowly.

DESERT ROSE

Mrs Fuselli acquired her name
with a husband long since discarded.

Fuselli – Madam? – no, 'Mrs'
is better. A touch of mystery.
No clink of amber beads.

'Does anybody know a Jim?'
Those pious brick halls, smelling of dust,
stale tea, gas, and very faintly of feet.

'Does *anybody* know a Jim?'
Small men, their stranded hair
combed over pink scalps, proffer
mousy velvet collection bags.

'Jim? He's wanting to make contact..'
She keeps a tight rein. Raw response
is banished, whimpering to dust balls
under the stacking chairs.

Mrs Fuselli *could* do the tarot,
still has a crystal ball stashed against
hard times but is 'more *spiritual*' now,

has a brass plate. Cleverer
than she knows, her only trick
cutting out clues from the woolly flocks
of longing in her clients' eyes.

'It's my Steve' says Mrs Clark.
'He's missing.'

My Steve, how his baby skin
used to pink and smart. 'You

will take your sun lotion,
won't you?' 'Bloodyhellmum!
Gonna have a bit more to do
than worry about sunburn!
Yeah, ok, I'll put the Ambre Solaire
in me kit.Don't *worry* – ok?'

My Steve, couldn't hurt
a fly. Tears in his eyes
when his dog died, a sucker
for hard luck stories,
wearing his pressed combats
like branded sports gear.

'Mrs Clark, if, and I say *if*
Steven has passed over, I must
project my spirit across to him,
and I can't do that without some
feel for what he's like.Can I?'

Reluctantly Mrs Clark ferrets
in her bag. 'Steve and his mates.'
Passes a colour photo, three young
men in civvies, three pints of beer,
self-conscious, legs planted
like capital A' s, identical grins.

'Mrs Clark,'firmly 'we are
going to have five minutes silence
thinking of Steven and giving him
the chance to *come through.'*

Silence settles like the sift
of sand and Mrs Fuselli's
dry lizard scuttling thoughts
grow still with alarm.

3

Bullets whanging off the wheel arch.
Snipers? Ambush? Steve with his bag
of spanners has never fired a shot
but looked with melancholy
satisfaction at crumpled houses,
burnt out tanks. Hoped
it didn't hurt. WHANG! The driver's
head a red mist. OUT bellows
the sergeant, UNDER the jeep.

Silence. Then like a roar of kettledrums,
shouts, screams, thud of approaching feet.
No time to feel. Fear a compacted
snowball in his belly. Faces, fierce
as hawks without a blind,
ordinary faces ground sharp
by hunger. A man with yellow eyes
yanks him to his feet.
No time to feel the terrible sorrow
of a black-crossed prey.
Steel nuzzles his soft buzz cut.

Silence.

Grain upon grain, accreting
like a desert rose. Mrs Fuselli
never knew that death was so
silent. Never knew how it filled
your skull with nothing at all.

Mrs Clark watches Mrs Fuselli's
face slide
like candle wax:

stiffly she rises and walks away.

ALONE IN THE THUNDEROUS HOUSE

Beethoven and the loud
silence of nesting birds
outside the double glazing

and the smaller silences of gaps
between sheets, towels, pillowcases,
lying down quietly in the striped sun
from the blind

as if they had never been centrifuged
or ironed flat and the resigned
dumbness of tins in the cupboard
waiting to be cut ...

I could go on. As if silence
was *for* something, as if the silence
at the heart of music had a purpose
which once you knew,

could be suffered and that
would be OK, because *for*
leads out of nothing towards
something – doesn't it?

Dumb terror of Cumae.
But the supplicant had only to wait,
while Sybil, dried up raisin in her basket,
fragment of brittle wax

in the goddess's ear,
never knew between
speech and silence
which word

would scatter the ashes
of her voice.

SHOKAT DANCING

She's humming, the heart
of a brown flower.
Pixels blaze erratically:
off, on, pick up the DNA
of music, scribbled in the air.

Cumbersome with arthritis,
its creaking bulk, she moves
restively, turns in this extra overcoat.
Inside Shokat, never slim
but curved as a deer's haunches,
picking its path on slender legs.

She's cooked a mountain
of rice, steaming lamb,
thrusts her way, plates high,
through the neat Dutch room,
the blond women.
Already the dance
is waiting.

Pale squares on the wall,
daughter left behind,
husband, son, a continent away.
Here in the neat box
of her asylum, Shokat
laughs, turns up the music,
shivers like ice from nape
to buttocks on a hot day.

She begins, pinching
the stuff of her skirt
as if it were velvet or silk
and courtly, away from
her hips. Vibrating now,
strong throat arched, head
thrown back over the shaking
column, feet in turned over shoes,

nimble, precise, active as bees.
Shokat, dancing in her white desert
peoples it with light,
called up from the brave spin
of her haunches.

We can't go, where she has been,
or follow when the music stops
and she turns out of it –
easy and every day
as a body turning in bed
from sleep.

WELLINGTON BOOTS

My god is wearing wellington boots
and a sacking apron.

Her cracked brown thumbs, dried
by soil, ruthlessly

weed out drooping seedlings while
firming up the strong.

You should see her prune! Like
a high-speed gazelle

with steel jaws, her clippers graze
each shivering stem.

Don't think she belongs to a kinder
sex. One smudge of her strong

thumb, a continent's gone, the bright grain
blistered while others groan

with pleasurable juice. A global
view. Her flocks are trees,

all soul, no brain, easy to drive
through the fast crannies of the world,

long outlasting the perishable heat
of mammals.

Did I invent her? No. But I hope
as she sits by the evening

shadow of the potting shed in a breath
of cool night-scented stock,

peaceably rolling a fag, she won't
reject

my liturgy,
red berries in a jar.

HIVE

Beekeepers wearing their ridiculous gloves
sometimes stroke
the furry coats of bees

when they want them to move,
to coalesce in a fat, glistening
lump on a stick

and go where they don't want to.
And the bees can't resist.
They shudder and purr,

as close as bees come to laughing.
Coercion or symbiosis?
Does anything matter but honey?

But the purpose of bees is
not honey, the amber breast–milk
of flowers.

Careless as a skeleton leaf brazing
its cathedral window tracery
on November pavements,

they spend the last of love,
mysterious harvest, heavy
with laughter from the hive.

ANGEL AND VIRGIN
Hans Memling

He's looking at her, as if to say
'You won't forget the sausages
this time?' – that heavenly intimacy
somewhere between an angel
and a pair of herrings.

They look so much alike,
related as brother and sister,
or bride and groom, whose instinct
is to pair with like,
not knowing they'll end

twinned as an old man
in a pub with dog, a joke
but faithful. It's human
to want our mysteries to arrive
in a hush of powerful wings

like the divine curve
of resting feathers
between these two,
but deep in the germ
of holy sperm,

somewhere between prick
and heart, a carnal bud
disrupts that formal garden,
rueful and necessary
as a fart.

BECOMING

'Tell Chiel to bring me 500 guilders.'
What can he possibly want with
all that cash? We sit, his plastered leg
pointing towards the dusk. Outside
a fountain wilting in the rain.

He's nodding, doing difficult sums,
connected in his head to hospitality,
its cost, paying his dues.

Upstairs I'd put his underwear away,
seen how his suits had strained a seam
to fit the new curve of his back.

'Papa' I say 'your toes – zoals een
regenbouw.' 'Heh!' he is delighted,
my pidgin Dutch 'jij leert het wel!'
Evening, colouring like a bruise
fills us with quiet. His hand shoots
out. 'Every day', he says, 'I forget.
What happens? Who comes?
I don't know.
But I remember *you*.'

No ghost of charm, a full 500
watts burn blue in his eyes.

He's getting smaller, but not dwindling.
Even his clothes give up the struggle,
become a second skin.

'Don't forget,
500 guilders!' No. I may not do it,
but I won't forget
how reduction means
a richer soup,

how this homeopathic dose
his self, becoming
more himself
becomes
him.

LOST PROPERTY

She's lost her memory.
Doesn't know where she put it –
keeps casting for its scent,
rattling cupboard doors.

Was it a hatbox or suitcase?
Which? Scuffed corners, cardboard
showing through, a bent brass key
on string?

Lost, lost, bus tickets, feathers,
hatpins, a broken pen, an unstrung
necklace, her confirmation prayer book,
the vicar's spidery hand,
letter of reference from the cook,
her mother, hoping this finds her
as it leaves them at home.

No wedding lines.
A photo, bilious yellow as nicotine,
her on a stiff self-conscious khaki arm,
a black framed notice, creased,
some folded grey suede gloves.

Snippets of hats, she loved them. Petals
of artificial silk on blackened wire,
violets, peonies, roses, a liturgy of colour,
worn to church in hopes of rising
not again but now.

No passport either. A day return
to Scarborough. A weekend, later,
in Southend. She's lost it, lost it.

14

Under the pile, a birth certificate,
no father. A round dark head,
her breast a fountain choked too soon.

Doesn't know where she put it.
Knows it was a suitcase,
handle shaped for carrying.

She's lost her memory but not
its weight and shape and pain.

HEARTH PRAYER

As I get older I begin to pray.
Not *please.* Too late for that.
Or even *thankyou*. Irrelevant,

though closer. They sit,
the focus of my prayers,
their lumpy feet easefully

spread on my hearth,
potato faces turned to
the fire. They hawk

sizzling phlegm into the coals
wipe their noses on a sacking apron,
settle their bellies on spread thighs

and belch in anticipation
of pot herbs sweet cakes
and wine. How well we rub

along together. No
thin ideals or meagre virtue,
no terror. If I threw

them in the yard
birds would nest
in their mossy cracks.

But when they intercept
a look from me to you,
one that says, against all

evidence, *forever*, I know
from their kindly, lowered eyes
they understand irony,

though mockery runs off
their plain and serviceable spirits
like water

on a newborn's skull.

MARS VISITING

At first it was almost like a party.
All the neighbourhood lights were on,
but low, some rooms in darkness, dim
figures coming and going on balconies
as we waited.

No over-excitement. We were secure
as planetary beings round our sun
of dailiness, interrupted only by a visitor
at whom we could stare without
rudeness.

No moon. Little clouds. Ruffles
of sleeping bird sound. A neighbourhood
cat. Occasional glints of lesser stars.
Then Mars visiting, through
a rent in the clouds.

Bright as a plane bound for Schiphol
but softer, steadier, more domestic,
it seemed he burned for us.

Then with a flare so bright that every
colour lived and died in it,
he slipped sideways and down
the sky like a red hot
zip undoing.

Under her frill of cloud the moon
lurched and fell on her back.
Now, we wait in the aftershock,
where nothing happens
that can be felt or faintly imagined,

dumb as stars.

CONFERENCE GARDEN

A small landscape.
One palm tree, its trunk thicker than
three nuns.

Faint sharpness of quince,
memory brittle as a camellia's
sepia frill.

Now a ramble of weeds rushing
lusher than skirts, fleshy petals
dropping, the quiet click

of bird's feet.
Forty women rusting somewhere
through the greying rags

of their habits, while blokes
in jeans heave bulging barrows,
slap and stroke new plaster.

This way the new wing.
Loo, cafeteria – used to be the refectory –
hall, candles extinguished. Sealed

with salt. If it rains the walls
and windows
will sweat plainsong.

Nuns who wrestled their hearts
square to fit this garden
or fitted like small native birds

in the stitched borders
and loved like leached marble,
or bravely,

as some sturdy crimson rambler,
or not at all.

An equal reward.

IN THE FRAME

Windows are the frame that has chosen me.
A kind of ghostly architectural grid
is etched on my retina, even where no bricks and mortar stand.

Some people choose faded gilt or limed oak.
For them a frame is a designer accessory,
its necessary function so well disguised as personal choice

that they don't see what has escaped round
the straight, exigent edges, or if they do
they know it can't be valuable. It wasn't bought.

For me, looking out at the wild, lush garden
where feral cats prowl and birds practise little
half-finished stanzas in their sleep,

or in, as families eat in lamplight, silently
opening their mouths for speech or food or kisses,
it is the wild, metasable state of glass,

its passionate atoms caught in the act of cooling
that keeps my blood from leaching.
As it would. If the glass broke.

I SPEAK THROUGH MY EAR

I speak through my ear
when my tongue is dumb
and nobody knows that these tiny
tinny creaks, small as grass growing
or the squeak of a hearing-aid battery fading,
are my voice.

Encochleated sounds, whispered
through a shell, a vanishing-point rumble
as one grain of sand falls,
or the silence of silver settling
on a film.

Why? Because even atoms grumble,
perpetually dancing,
and silence itself is stitched together
in a flash of submicroscopic mirrors
whose amplified wink
is sound of honey growing
or ash after fire,

so I must, mustn't I, as Sybil must,
until I learn to take as beloved guest
the head of her implacable visitor
on my breast.

THE PLAINNESS OF HER FACE

Today she sees her plain face
in the mirror. Yesterday
she found the mailbox

crackling with ozone.
Enough lines drawn.
A time for folding

shadows. They occupy
so little space. Less
than light in a cup,

her cup set down,
a neat full stop.
Refusing metaphor

she shelves it.
Refusing irony,
she takes her keys

buffed by handling,
glowing in the year's
first sun

and door ajar,
drops them down
the shaft.

'Missis, Missis' says the beggar
in the street, mittened claws
dark from handling

pence. She spills
her gaping purse.
The day

has lambs tail scudding
clouds. Her face
is plain

as a hill inured to tricks
of light. Days like a dictionary
of leaves

have come and gone.
Nothing revokes
the plainness of her face.

LIVING BELOW SEA-LEVEL

'Life is always a defense against grief. You're below sea level, like the Netherlands'. Harold Brodkey

Diamond pin, chalk stripe,
ambivalent as a razor sharp
trousercrease,

your cornrow hair all tidy.
You have grown up,
Pollyanna.

Anna is more svelte,
Polly possible, but not quite
how you see

yourself now that you have
no jelly sandwiches hidden
in your briefcase

and you spell Futures
with a capital. One
thing, though, is always

the same. That smile,
aching with certainty
that everything you can't change

will be fine if, sunny enough,
you fade out shadow.
Your old blue dress

is now a polishing rag.
Once it was a sky-blue doll's
skirt. Before that

you wore it,
before the white daisies
became bleached dots,

when they still had sepals
and stamens.
Do you remember slipping

through the pines like a piece
of sky?
You left the sun frying up the blue

and took your own slice of light
deep down the path
of silent red needles,

white socks flashing, brown knees
twinkling, safe in your blue.
It's only stories, you said,

not real, when you came out
of the forest, blinking,
your white socks stained rusty red,

one sandal strap broken.
I wanted to scour your freckles
off with sandstone.

I wasn't frightened.
I watched the little bird
bob in your adam's apple

and my hand trembled
as I brushed the coarse
red needles off your back.

Now you are grown
and have given up orphanhood
and your skinny red plaits

have a grave of their own
and you live below sea-level,
on the flat.

It's possible to take ordinary
precautions and calculated risks
against the sea

but no one can tell you how
or why, precisely, you must be so
careful of the sky.

TRAM

The same well-scrubbed, plain light
Vermeer let fall on the bumpy
forehead of his maid, milk
from her jug blue as a newborn's
twisted cord.

Sun shimmies up the tallest
brick, lines each gable
sober gold. Rattling on medusa
braids our tram wriggles its sturdy
hips, as light lifts out,
sharp as a glass-cutter,
each topmost pane we pass.

Disappearing vee of soft, scarred,
well-used light, deep as a peepshow,
finds fleetingly a fat man's hairy belly,
singlet creased as he scratches,
a child's bear propped by the window,
the sudden filmy yawn of opened doors,
kitchen shelves a sly wink of jewels.

Clear as the knobbled shine
on maid, mistress, braided milk,
each still-life shows
as the tram rocks
from patinated shadow
to sun,

how light works
earthing epiphanies.

WHERE ARE MY BONES?

All the little dogs in the Vondelpark
know if they keep on looking
and are not too distracted
by any one thing – yellow balls, aromatic pee,
crotches just out of reach, empty polystyrene
containers, stained golden,

they will find the bone of bones.
So they jump on their coil-sprung legs
from delightful task to task,
are selectively deaf when the *baas* with a fearsome
silver whistle means business and balance
love and disobedience

in ways we need to remember.
Even very old little dogs
don't walk but lift each cork
lined foot and hop onto the next
with a tiny residual spring.
Their noses, which need a soft polish

to supple them up,
never abandon the search.
The oiled and languorous lovers
who knot themselves like baskets of snakes
in the sun, the sweaty runners
hammering with their heavy feet,

the anxious parents of children spilling
like Smarties – and still too much
like little dogs – the bone-tired junkies,
dark rings swallowing their eyes,
boys snapping pheromones like beer-can
tags, they could – not *learn* – but let, perhaps?

the one question off its lead
along with the little dogs
who follow its enticing smells
and roll over grinning.
No more running in packs
with bared teeth. There *is* a question
whose answer is buried
in the rich, careless litter of its asking.

TON

Somewhere in a small Dutch town
Ton will be lying with his kind body

hidden in its best suit, that slight
list, as much from listening

as an earlier stroke, stowed away.
Jan will have seen that he

and the flowers are perfect,
since perfect is what he always

wanted and the dog – great, daft
fellow, long on pedigree

short on brains – will do
what dogs, who have skipped

evolution, can do and grieve
from a bottomless heart.

According to the little fried eggs
on the weather charts,

today will be sheeted there
with early silver and young gold,

as it is here. Every death
gives those who are left

one more day.
Thank you Ton.

ENCAUSTIC
Picture of an iris by Lex Goes.

Yellow, edited with a dribble of egg-yolk orange,
raw canvas sewn with waxy pollen,
and the tissue-thin, pressed, clear
petals, hammered into the wax,
heavy strokes, brush, knife, spatula.

Its shape – only as iris-shaped as that glimpse you catch
of a foreign woman with an anxious face in a dark shop window
but know it is yourself – so slow and molten
and iris-like in its folded back, crimsonly purple transparencies.
Dissected, it bleeds out its blueblack blood.

If this is death it is more collected than life.
Iconic faces burned in wax for tomb-burial live
their accidental resurrection. This is no accident.
The crocus drip, off-centre, puns
bawdy, bee-fumbled pistils

but no more piercing joke exists than the casual
knitting of DNA. Except its decay.

If asked to kneel for a flower
I should blush but here,
from the furled corm
to the bruised petals,
is all my ungracious kneeling
packed in.

COME BACK, GORDON

Gordon, I never liked the name, but he was second hand
before I got him. He had wobbly ankles.
All his stuffing had gone to his feet, which bulged
like old-lady feet at the nursing home
where my mother cleaned
and I pushed old ladies back in their chairs
when her back was turned
and they tried to get up –
heaven help me – me next!

Gordon Bear in his mousey, red knitted knickers,
smelling as if he'd spent the night between
some other kid's legs, while underneath
a bitter, earthy quality – old dust? glue? kapok? –
spoke gravely, though his squeak was dead.
Did I love him? No, he was necessary to me
and taught me speechless lessons,
how a pinch of love can cover the taste of need,
spice in a curry of doubtful origin,
and how the needy suck their hydroponic diet,
and thrive quietly

till you want to kick them. And Gordon
needed me. You could tell from his beer bottle
glass eyes. We used to look in the mirror,
together soulfully, two sets of bear-ish eyes,
his fur balding, my plaits scraped back,
and I would worry out a curl from
my flattened hair. Gordon approved
of this hint of wildness, you could tell,
but it didn't save him in the end.
Too old to give away, he went in the bin.

Dear Gordon, you can come back now,
if you like. I don't want to be cruel anymore,
now I know the difference between your baldness
and my whiskers. I don't need you any more,
Gordon – or if I do, it doesn't much matter.
It isn't a competition for your monitor's badge,
is it? Who cares from what strange plant
the long shadow of tenderness falls?

CRACKS IN THE PAVEMENT

You **musn't** tread on them.
You jump. Sometimes
a tuft of chickweed,
glossed in the wind
of your passing, deceives.
Your plimsoll lands
square on a hidden crack.

Nothing you can offer then
except your fierce
begging chicken-ribbed chest.

Don't smack me...don't let me
be awake...don't let me be
found out...I will be good...

Fists white and waxy
as small, knobbed potatoes,
eyes stitched black, scrunched
shut as a rag doll's face.

Let me come top...have curly hair
let her be friends with me...

Shrine of magpie pebbles,
chipped, faded jackstones, a glass
marble seeded with bubbles, clear
as fish's breath and pliant daisies.
*Please,*they say, *please.*
Less often *thanks* is needed.

Later, so holy people teach,
is answer, just as *yes* or *no.*
Oh-yeah??stuffit-up-yer-jacksi-then!

36

Don't say it aloud.
Ant-like columns of print
from bible paper will crawl
and stain of windows spread
like a crimson birthmark
on your skin.

No *please*, no *thank you*,
no cracks to jump,
just tree-ring years, forcing
a painful space, as pavements buckle.

The whole stem-cell of this world and stars
grown gnarled and scarred,
an old root vegetable,

and everywhere people bowed, only
ever, under the homely, necessary weight
of their own hearts.

ELEPHANT AUNTS

My Aunt only knew the title,
my best book,
the one I begged for every night,
not that I called her Elephant Aunt
because her legs, stout and shapeless,
armchair thighs, bun feet,
recalled the Aunts' comfortable
grey, wrinkled ankles.

Wholly benign,
the Elephant Aunts.
Sisters. One wore spectacles.
Both had kind little
piggy eyes. You knew
their trunks would soothe,
like cool wet velvet,
tip to nape.

My Aunt —
once in a draper's
I saw a bolt of flannel
bound down the mahogany
counter like a heifer,
dangerous run-away cloth.
You might long
for the wise upholstery
of a lap. You got cake
on a plate and its consequences.

Planted. Not a word I knew,
but the Elephant Aunts' legs
thrust up, carrying the weight
of their great grey bellies and their
flowered pinnies, while rooting
them in jungle earth.

Set, my Aunt was, I
learned later, though
more like blancmange
than concrete. How
the Elephant Aunts
would have dignified
my bones with kisses,
a child not theirs,

owning only the short-sighted
kindness of their clever hearts,
not bothering about *blood
will out.* Lucky I believed
in them first, vast grey
benignancies, in my father's
bed-time voice,

before I learned that *thicker
than water* hissed at the tea table
wasn't a cup of weak tea,
but how you described
who I would never be.

THE MAN ON A BIKE

'Tell me! What did he say...?'

She means *'What did he* **do?***'*
She'll ask me soon, but I won't say.

Coals shift in our tiny grate,
little blue hisses, sulphurous farts,
smell like wet horses.

I'm standing in a chipped enamel bowl,
water gone cold and scummy,
red sliver of Lifebuoy, an extra finger
poking as she scrubs a little harder.

*'You'll have to say if you saw him,
the policeman wants to know.'*
She soaps between my legs so hard
my buttocks set
like bannister knobs.

'Course I won't tell her,
she smacked my bum only for taking
sixpence from Uncle Ted.
Silly old man on a bicycle's worth
more than a slap, I expect.

How did he hold his bike so still,
one hand on the sit-up-and-beg handlebars,
the other tenting his long mac,
hem draggling its chain,
poised on two wheels
like a wave waiting to fall,
his little purple thing
less naked than his face?

Our clock ticks, its sturdy
oak overcoat humming,
before the next strike.

*'Six o'clock. Your Dad'll
make you tell.'* Minutes stretch,
frail, unbroken Yankee chewing gum.
I make my eyes opaque as chocolate –
bedtime at last.

Trust me.
He doesn't say it, words are scarce.
On ration. Makes soft little mumbles,
nudges with his voice, furrows
his freckled forehead, its white band
where his trilby sits.

Dong – quarter past six, he's missed his news.
Must be important. Hasn't had his tea.
A gilded rim round the soft, washed out
blur of our bedroom curtains. Bird cries
of kids in the street. Daylight out there.

Wants me to say, something, anything,
not too much, my mother's shadow
twisting its hands on the landing. *'He didn't…?'*
This I can do. *'No, Dad.'* Their bed, its muffled cave
of sighs and groans you're not supposed to hear

gives me the clue. *'I didn't see anything.'*
Eyes soft and grateful he tucks me in,
his hard hands sheathed.

My mother thrums, neglected steam.
She knows I am my Daddy's girl, while she,
guardian of the grit in our family gizzard,
grinds different stones.

ASH

Poured into his boxy jacket
like asphalt smoking in its wooden form,
a fine rain sweating his face,
his hands bulging with tension,
like rabbits in a sack,
he thrust at me
out of the tarmac waste,
Willesden bus garage
on a cold spring night.

I was nineteen, had been to see
Friendly Persuasion in Harlesden,
had my head full of Pat Boone
and Quaker bonnets –
although my bones thrilled
like teeth after ice-cream
to the smell of privet,
laid dust and faintly imagined spring
flowers. Besides, I was a Catholic.

And a virgin, so when he begged
in a voice stripped of everything
but its last human molecule
'come home with me'
I jumped away. Not
because he was black
but male – and not like Pat Boone
or my father – and because
of the fine coating of ash in his voice.

O man from the bus garage,
I am so sorry. Although
I remember the terrible ache
in your face, I couldn't have done it.
Not then, not now,
though I know too well
how sorrow borrowed from what you
can't – or won't – assuage becomes a debt,
if wise, you understand you can't redeem,

but wear
as quietly as ash signing your skin.

A BONE

O, my heart, my mother: from the Egyptian Book of the dead.

'I've got a bone in me leg!'
my mother said
and she wouldn't budge,
no she would not.

My first lesson
on the waterfall force
of will,

and that small space,
breathing wet rock
and ferns, where the water
couldn't come.

But you can't stay
crouched

or rheumatism will be
your lot and that will
search out your own bones.

Other organs need bones.

O, my heart, my mother,
how else will you remember
when memory has leaked out
of your sack?

I have got a bone in my heart.

BARE FACED

'*Well,*' said my mother, '*that's*
a barefaced lie if *ever* I heard one!'

I see now, her voice had the kind of poetry
that drives you wild.

You thrash and struggle
till you solve the mixed messages.

Bare is bad, barefaced is worse,
and lies are worst of all.

Like false eyelashes,
bare can cover up

what you do and what
you don't want known.

The strip between bikini
line and breast

is not like winter woods
where each leaf aches to fall.

I don't want to wear my nakedness
like fashion. It's harder won.

It is my very bones before they strip.

It's the face I wear before
my thoughts can cover it

through learning to lie
bare faced by you.

SLEEPING TOGETHER

Our bodies chattering quietly together
like starlings, prepare
as each cell settles on the branches of our sleep.

We are used to this now, no longer find
a ripe fart or morning's sour breath an embarrassment,
or passion an interruption

any more than a floating crisp packet
disrupts the flow of broad water.
You lay your head in the hollow of my arm-pit.

Time's up. Now comes the small animal
shuffle of turning, breast to back,
belly to buttocks

and later in the conversation that velcro
kiss of sweating skin
unsticking

and brief pause for the cooler reaches
of sleep. 'What did you dream?' you ask.
You felt my hand heavy as a small anchor

on your thigh and briefly our boat
rocked with a small shock
outside of language. If growing old

is giving up what you know you can say,
then not only our days aquire patina.
Our nights deepen transparently,

our speech, like a mute swan's
is more the proud
or tender flexing of feathers

outside the lexicon
and learned
as water drinks reflection.

FOSSIL FUEL

All the little girls in white communion dresses
kneeling in my dark school playground,
playing a fierce pattacake game.

Silently the Rolls stops between goalposts.
Out slips the bride,
gleaming like a walrus tusk.

You sense she was handed onto our dim yard
from deeper darkness. All the little girls
have forgotten this morning's Jesus

in their play. As I will forget this morning's
dream – but its flavour, like a deep smell of fruit,
will drift for a while

in my archive, where dreams pile and compact,
bleeding their sepias into each other.

Like turf in the making,
a rich prehistory settles and sighs.

It will burn well.

THE BLEEDING KEY

She's late, heels clacking,
empty streets, silent fanlights,
a downward thrust of rigid
calves, a gleam of brass
in glossy doorways.

Why no taxi? Because her
gut would roil on the vinyl seats,
and here moist air clings to her face
like half forgotten silk,
because birds in their sleep
practise songs drowned out in daytime,
tiny glass bead threads chinking
in a darkened square.

Cacophony of heels.
She slips off her shoes,
risks dog shit, gum and sputum.
Cool spreads like spilled sea,
slakes her dry feet.
Crisp little chrysalis leaf curls
nudge her instep. Now the gate.

Black wrought iron,
velvet with rain, swings
generously wide, halts with a silent
shudder. The moon fades
to dimmer-switch darkness.
Sudden familiar blue
fluorescence blares.

Dazzled she drops her shoes,
fumbles her soft skin bag,
her hand groping its silken
lining. Her key lies,
sharp, shiny teeth in a pool.

Wet warmth. Slippery.
She pulls it out. Shakes.

A black drop
collects on its silver snout,
falls on the bleached
path. She stoops, a careful
forefinger, not yet trembling,
stirrs. Smears.

She drives the key
into its slot. Silent light in the hall.
A first visceral tremble.

Red? Quick as a threatened
snake, she flings the key,
it skids on polished wood,
is swallowed by a crimson rug.
A clumsy stumbling run.
The kitchen. Stained fingers flush
white porcelain pink. She gags.
Thin, clotted bile, tapwater, silence.

*What is it? It can't be. I must
be hallucinating* – sudden rush
of candour – *drunk. I'll throw
it out on the rug.* Adrenaline. *No
you dont't, it's a Bokhara!* Drags
herself against invisible wires
shaking with messages. Squats.
Gingerly lifts a braided edge.

Her Yale lies quietly.
One red drop quivers
on its' pointed nose.

Stop trembling! Out to the kitchen.
Marigold gloves. Perfectly
rational explanation. O god
where shall I put it? She can't

face the sink, the bin seems
all wrong...Got it! In the fridge
wrapped in plastic. There
may its wounds slow
and congeal, its vivid weeping
cease. A small corpse
wrapped in a Sainsbury's bag.
Harmless as a pound of sausages.

Sleep rises like water
withheld,

presses behind her eyes,
aches,

drily absent. She turns,
plunges.

Gentuljeesusmeek'nmild
Lookerponalittulchild-n'if
I dieforeI wake – every night

before her toes reach the bottom
of the bed, she must say it,
before sleep and its friends

get her. Mugged by the Sandman
at last her dreams are threaded
by the late crystal chime

51

of birds, practising, practising
in their sleep. She is in the garden
in her shirred elastic swimsuit,

digging a hole like a frantic
puppy, just outside the henrun.
The hens, with every ruffled shrug,

say *Calm! Too hot to fuss.*
But they have only to lay eggs.
No corpse to bury.

She found him on the scratched bottom
of his cage, little persian arabesques
of birdshit, split black and white

seeds, his empty china water pot
and the tiny writing of his twig feet
said *dead*. She knows dead.

When her Mum comes back
she'll thrust him into her hand,
like the day old chicks,

so many gobbetts of cooling meat
she'd to touch to learn 'dead'. *Quick!*
into the bag, shut the cage door,

don't wait for his eyes to film, for
What *have you done?* Later, later.
Now is a throat, a hole in the ground.

Now the moon pours
its black and white leaves
through the slats of her blinds.

Dry as the feathers she feels
in her hands, her heart beats,
small peas of gravel
shaken on a drum.

In the kitchen the fridge groans.
Its undigested load, designer food
and blood,
will need more ice.

She's stepping through a mirror,
through the dark papery circles
round her own eyes,
dry as a hoop for a circus pony.

Stephanie, stephanotis, O'Farrell,
I longed for your dark red plait,
thicker than an anchor cable,
to touch my skinny wrist.

So long ago, my small
scarred heart ploughed under,
waiting to glimpse
the slow buttercup

sheen of your breast.
Carry your bags?
Wait at the station?
***Particular** friendships,*

says Mother Monica,
are contrary to the will
of Our Lord – and what would
*Our Lady say to something **unfresh**?*

What
is the one smell you can never forget,
Smoke? bread? or the quiet

subdued softness of her skin?
Wet dog, plimsolls, cheesy

corduroy boy-knickers?
Comic olfactory clichés,

sharp as the squeak of blackboard
chalk, dissect the nerve

pleasure/pain. But grass,
timelessly resurrecting,

and the empty spice-bottle dryness
of privet leavings and dust,

grass, parrot green through pavements,
fermenting in toppling heaps,

in hosepipe-ban time
smelling like a wounded river bed,

drunk on rain,
singing its deep green intoxicated song,

grass, close-cut as a gentleman's hair,
where the marquee gently lifts its skirts,

drowning hot flesh, aftershave, finest wool,
dressed silk,

grass, that blew through the church door
as their looks,

freighted with contractual promises
weighed to the last scruple,

exchanged betrayal, him for a trophy
cash-down,

her for a landlocked inlet, safe
from that other terrible green resurrection.

What is it that beats
like a fading
bird's pulse,

is ragged as a hangnail,
shocks like a deep
scratch on a polished table?

Whose is that thin
silvery voice,
its grain coming clear?

Weeeuuu weeeuuu weeeuuu
What? What? The key? No.
Only a car alarm. White noise.

Heavy, a woollen blanket,
sleep, clings in dark folds.

But her eyes snap wideawake,
dry as laburnum pods.

Children,
fragile bones bent in canopic jars,
sealed with unwrinkled wax.

'We're designer accessories' Harry said to me
when I wouldn't let him paint.

Milly wasn't so clever. She just got pregnant.
We wouldn't let her

ruin her life, of course. She doesn't
visit often, not now she's married.

At least you could rely on her father
to do the right thing.

I kept my side of the bargain,
didn't see much of Mum and Dad

after our wedding. No loss for her.
Dad was a bit puzzled at first...

and *I kept my looks...and more than*
he *can say, I was faithful,*

though sometimes a look, lashes
on a cheek...

Silently her dead shift in the cellar.
and sigh,

pile of discarded carapaces.
Deliberately she sleeps.

'What you gonna do when you
grow up?' 'Gonna be

a n'archaeologist.' Older, in battered
boater and school tie

she sees through gallery glass,

black breath on limestone walls where sconces
flamed and burning butterfly colours.

Deep in her own face, traces of ochre,
crimson, transparent gold

and mummy cases, two fragile boats facing,
balanced round the sleep of the dead.

Breath of the museum
like dried tears in a bottle.

She steps through the fresco
past the duck, started from faded grass,

past the dog straining its leash.
She's pulled by a divining quiver

from her key in its cold burrow,
thirsty for its north. Black

as an ashlar tomb slab, a dark
so deep it drowns.

When Stephen
fell down with his heart

and I just looked, but couldn't
touch, was it as black as this

for him? My little Dad,
so shrunken in his striped pyjamas,

wanted to hold my hand. My finger tipped
his wrist. I never knew

a look, a touch can make your own
blood blossom one last time.

Nor does she know how sadness,
a gift ordinary as water,
nothing you can claim, nothing
you can spoil,

creates a threshhold
so under the iron horse shoe,
magnetic doorway,
each molecule reverses.

Still dark, but dark as a lidded eye.
She sees the mummy case,
soft gleam of bitumen.

WaaaaAAAH! AlaaaAAA! A red cry,
furious, robust. *IwannabreastbottlemiiiLK!*
GIMME!

Brrum, brrrum, bruUUM.
LemmeOUTlemmeOUT.
Heels on the empty shell.

A quick staccato rattle, fading now,
WaaaaA, alaaaA, a fading cry.
I don't believe it! Dreaming.

Clutching her rosary of unbelief.
WaaaaaH.. Smaller than a day old chick's peep.

She blushes in the black shade, kicks
the priceless catafalque to splinters.

*God! What a night! What time
is it?* Mundane, hungover
morning.

She stretches,
feels each joint has sprung,
feels too an ache of absence
in her breast, pleasant
as a bird-shaped empty nest,
or hand still cupped for water.

Water! The fridge! The key!
She runs to the kitchen

unafraid, she doesn't wonder
why. Clunk, the fridge door
opens, a greasy pack, faint smell,
meconium and blood.

The key, inert and cool.

She drops
its plastic wrapping in the bin,
wipes her hand absently
on her slub-silk thigh.

She will carry this baby like a sore thumb,
a puckered rose in her side,

hidden as the secret life of fields
beneath their surfaces

or the moment of consent
so braided in its source

it's never seen, though all we've been
and might have been,

runs in its bed,

dangerous dreaming,
our only key
to home.

OTHER POETRY FROM SHOESTRING PRESS

POEMS Manolis Anagnostakis. Translated into English by Philip Ramp. A wide-ranging selection from a poet who is generally regarded as one of Greece's most important living poets and who in 1985 won the Greek State Prize for Poetry.
ISBN 1 899549 19 6   £8.95

HALF WAY TO MADRID: POEMS, Nadine Brummer Poetry Book Society Recommendation. ISBN 1 899549 70 6   £7.50

TESTIMONIES: NEW AND SELECTED POEMS Philip Callow. With Introduction by Stanley Middleton. A generous selection which brings together work from all periods of the career of this acclaimed novelist, poet and biographer. ISBN 1 899549 44 7
£8.95

TARO FAIR, Ian Caws
ISBN 1 899549 80 3   £7.50

THE WEIGHT OF COW, Mandy Coe.
ISBN 1 899549 97 8   £7.95

INSIDE OUTSIDE: new and selected poems Barry Cole. "A fine poet ... the real thing." Stand. ISBN 1 899549 11 0   £6.95

GHOSTS ARE PEOPLE TOO, Barry Coe.
ISBN 1 899549 93 5   £6.00

SELECTED POEMS Tassos Denegris. Translated into English by Philip Ramp. A generous selection of the work of a Greek poet with an international reputation.
ISBN 1 899549 45 9   £6.95

THE NEW GIRLS, Sue Dymoke.
ISBN 1 904886 00 0   £7.95

COLLECTED POEMS Ian Fletcher. With Introduction by Peter Porter. Fletcher's work is that of "a virtuoso", as Porter remarks, a poet in love with "the voluptuousness of language" who is also a master technician. ISBN 1 899549 22 6   £8.95

THE HOME KEY, John Greening.
ISBN 1 899549 92 7   £7.95

KAVITA, TF Griffin. ISBN 1 899549 85 4   £6.50

LONG SHADOWS: POEMS 1957–2000 JC Hall. ISBN 1 899549 26 9   £8.95

SEVERN BRIDGE: NEW & SELECTED POEMS, Barbara Hardy.
ISBN 1 899549 54 4   £7.50 Second Printing

A PLACE APART, Stuart Henson.
ISBN 1 899549 91 9   £7.95

CRAEFT: POEMS FROM THE ANGLO-SAXON Translated and with Introduction
and notes by Graham Holderness. Poetry Book Society Recommendation.
ISBN 1 899549 67 6 £7.50

ODES Andreas Kalvos. Translated into English by George Dandoulakis. The first English
version of the work of a poet who is in some respects the equal of his contemporary,
Greece's national poet, Solomos. ISBN 1 899549 21 8 £9.95

A COLD SPELL Angela Leighton. "Outstanding among the excellent", Anne Stevenson,
Other Poetry. ISBN 1 899549 40 4 £6.95

WISING UP, DRESSING DOWN: POEMS, Edward Mackinnon.
ISBN 1 899549 66 8 £6.95

TOUCHING DOWN IN UTOPIA: POEMS, Hubert Moore
ISBN 1 899549 68 4 £6.95 Second Printing

ELSEWHERE, Michael Murphy.
ISBN 1 899549 87 0 £7.95

MORRIS PAPERS: Poems Arnold Rattenbury. Includes 5 colour illustrations of Morris's
wallpaper designs. "The intellectual quality is apparent in his quirky wit and the skilful
craftsmanship with which, for example, he uses rhyme, always its master, never its
servant." Poetry Nation Review. ISBN 1 899549 03 X £4.95

THE ISLANDERS: POEMS, Andrew Sant ISBN 1 899549 72 2 £7.50

BEYOND THE BITTER WIND: Poems 1982–2000, Christopher Southgate.
ISBN 1 899549 47 1 £8.00

STONELAND HARVEST: NEW AND SELECTED POEMS Dimitris Tsaloumas. This
generous selection brings together poems from all periods of Tsaloumas's life and makes
available for the first time to a UK readership the work of this major Greek–Australian
poet.
ISBN 1 8995549 35 8 £8.00

AT THE EDGE OF LIGHT, Lynne Wycherley.
ISBN 1 899549 89 7 £7.95

For full catalogue write to:
Shoestring Press
19 Devonshire Avenue
Beeston, Nottingham, NG9 1BS UK
or visit us on www.shoestringpress.co.uk